AUG 2019

Marion Donovan
and the Disposable Diaper

By Virginia Loh-Hagan

21st Century
Junior Library

Published in the United States of America by
Cherry Lake Publishing
Ann Arbor, Michigan
www.cherrylakepublishing.com

Content Adviser: Kirsten Edwards, MA, Educational Studies
Reading Adviser: Marla Conn, MS, Ed., Literacy specialist, Read-Ability, Inc.

Photo Credits: © sirtravelalot/Shutterstock.com, Cover, 1; © Marion O'Brien Donovan Papers, Archives Center, National Museum of American History, Smithsonian Institution, 4; © Everett Collection/Shutterstock.com, 6; © WAYHOME studio /Shutterstock.com, 8; © Marion Donovan (US2575164-0)/United States Patent and Trademark Office/www.uspto.gov, 10; © Monkey Business Images/Shutterstock.com, 12; © MISS TREECHADA YOKSAN/Shutterstock.com, 14; © Ronnachai Palas /Shutterstock.com, 16; © Marion Donovan (US3620553-1)/United States Patent and Trademark Office/www.uspto.gov, 18; © Rawpixel.com/Shutterstock.com, 20

Library of Congress Cataloging-in-Publication Data has been filed and is available at catalog.loc.gov

Cherry Lake Publishing would like to acknowledge the work of The Partnership for 21st Century Skills.
Please visit *www.p21.org* for more information.

Printed in the United States of America
Corporate Graphics

CONTENTS

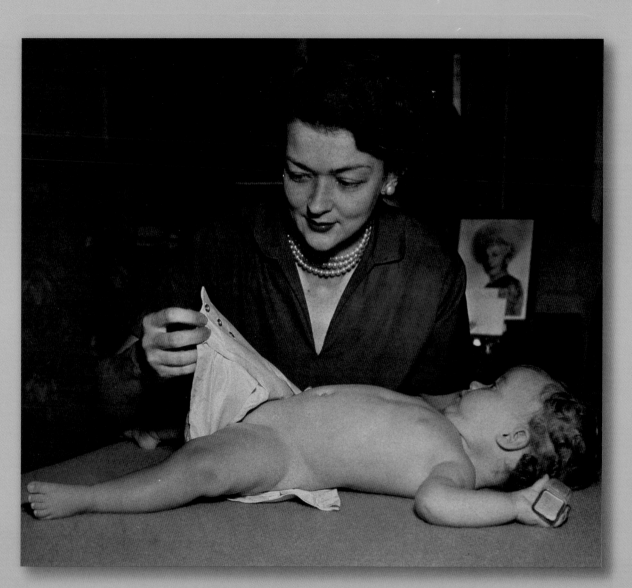

Donovan also worked with different companies
to help improve their products.

A Woman

Have you ever taken care of a baby? Think of all the things you have to do. First, you have to keep the baby safe. Second, you have to feed the baby. Third, you have to clean the baby. Babies pee and poop all day long. They need a lot of **diapers**.

Marion Donovan changed many diapers. But she didn't like the diapers during her time. She thought they could be improved. She invented the **disposable** diaper.

Many women at this time were homemakers.

Marion Donovan was born on October 15, 1917, in Indiana. She came from a family of inventors. Her father and uncle invented a machine that helped make car and gun parts. They were so successful that they opened a **factory** to make their machine.

Donovan's mother died when she was 7 years old. Because of this, Donovan spent a lot of time at her father's factory. She learned a lot from him.

She was always **tinkering**. She invented a tooth powder while in elementary school.

Inventors believe in making mistakes and learning from them.

Her father encouraged her. He showed her how to solve problems.

At 41 years old, she went to Yale University in Connecticut to get a master's degree in **architecture**. She was one of three women at Yale to do this during her time. She even designed her own house!

Ask Questions!

Talk to someone who takes care of children. Ask questions about what they do. Ask questions about their challenges.

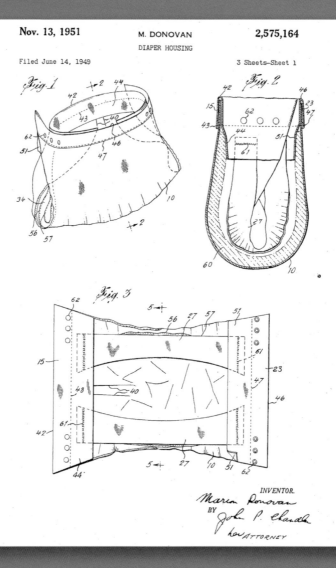

Her diapers had three snaps that could be
sized up as babies grew.

10

An Idea

Donovan had two children. This gave her real experience as a mother.

She had a problem with the diapers available for her children. They were used because they didn't leak. But they gave babies a rash. They dug into their legs and stomachs. She also didn't like cloth diapers. Cloth diapers made a mess. She wanted diapers that could hold liquid and let air in.

Today, diapers come in many different sizes.
They don't need snaps.

Donovan thought these were design failures. She wanted to fix these issues. She decided to invent her own diapers.

She used material from shower curtains and **nylon parachutes**. These materials are light and waterproof. They can be washed and reused. Donovan cut and sewed the materials together. She made them into diaper covers. Mothers could stuff them with **absorbent** paper. Donovan also used snaps, which made things faster and easier.

Donovan called her diaper cover the "Boater." Like a boat, it didn't leak. It also

Donovan measured many babies to create her invention.

looked like a boat. Donovan's invention made life easier for mothers. It also was more comfortable for babies. It was the first diaper to use snaps. It was also the first diaper to be waterproof.

Donovan's diaper covers were a hit. They sold out. Mothers everywhere wanted them. Donovan made a lot of money.

Think!

Think about names of inventions. Come up with different names. What would you call them?

Today, more mothers are becoming inventors.

A Legacy

Inventors are always thinking of ways to improve their inventions. Donovan was no different. Her next goal was to turn the Boater into a disposable diaper. She made a model and tried to sell it. But businessmen weren't interested. They said such diapers were not needed. But they were wrong.

Donovan's **legacy** can be seen now in the millions of disposable diapers used and

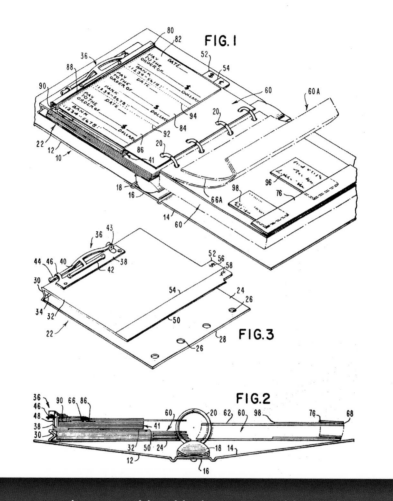

FIG. 1

FIG.3

FIG.2

She improved personal health, beauty, and household items.

18

sold every day. She was the first one to present the idea of a disposable diaper. Donovan knew what mothers needed because she was a mother.

She wanted to invent things that mattered. She had about 20 **patents**. She invented a cord used to zip up dresses. She invented a soap dish that drained into the sink. She invented a special type of

Create!

Create a new invention. Try to solve a problem in your house. Make life easier for your family.

Donovan was also a successful businesswoman.

dental floss. She invented a special clothes hanger.

She looked for ways to improve the simplest things. For her work, she was honored in the National Inventors Hall of Fame.

But she did more than just invent ideas. Donovan developed the inventions. She made machines to make her inventions. She marketed and sold the inventions. She did everything.

Donovan died on November 4, 1998. She paved the way for women inventors.

GLOSSARY

absorbent (ab-ZOR-buhnt) something that soaks up liquid easily

architecture (AHR-kih-tek-chur) the art or practice of designing and drawing plans for buildings

diapers (DYE-purz) pieces of absorbent material wrapped around a baby's bottom and between its legs to absorb and retain pee and poop

disposable (dih-SPOH-zuh-buhl) intended to be used once and then thrown away

factory (FAK-tuh-ree) a building or group of buildings where products are made in large numbers

legacy (LEG-uh-see) something handed down from one generation to another

nylon (NYE-lahn) a tough, light, stretchy material

parachutes (PAR-uh-shoots) cloth canopies that fill with air and allow people or heavy objects attached to them to descend slowly when dropped from the air

patents (PAT-uhnts) the rights from the government to use or sell inventions for a certain number of years

tinkering (TING-ker-ing) the act of trying to fix or make something

FIND OUT MORE

BOOKS

Caldwell, Stella A. *100 Women Who Made History: Remarkable Women Who Shaped Our World*. New York: DK Publishing, 2017.

Maggs, Sam. *Wonder Women: 25 Innovators, Inventors, and Trailblazers Who Changed History*. Philadelphia: Quirk Books, 2016.

Marsico, Katie. *Stinky Sanitation Inventions*. Minneapolis: Lerner Publications, 2014.

WEBSITES

The Atlantic—The Woman Who Invented Disposable Diapers
https://www.theatlantic.com/technology/archive/2014/10/the-woman-who-invented-disposable-diapers/381310
Learn more about how Donovan was unfairly treated as a woman inventor.

America Comes Alive—Inventor of the Diaper Cover and Forerunner of the Disposable Diaper
https://americacomesalive.com/2013/03/07/marion-obrien-donovan-1917-1998-inventor-of-the-disposable-diaper
Read a brief biography about Donovan's life and inventions.

INDEX

ABOUT THE AUTHOR

Dr. Virginia Loh-Hagan is an author, university professor, former classroom teacher, and curriculum designer. She's thankful for not having to change a lot of diapers. She lives in San Diego with her very tall husband and very naughty dogs. To learn more about her, visit www.virginialoh.com.